APR 2 9 2009

P9-ASN-703

WORLD BOOK'S
LIBRARY OF NATURAL DISASTERS

TORNADOES

WORLD
BOOK

a Scott Fetzer company
Chicago

www.worldbookonline.com

World Book, Inc.
233 N. Michigan Avenue
Chicago, IL 60601
U.S.A.

For information about other World Book publications, visit our Web site at
http://www.worldbookonline.com or call **1-800-WORLDBK (967-5325)**.

For information about sales to schools and libraries, call **1-800-975-3250 (United States);
1-800-837-5365 (Canada)**.

2008 revised printing

Library of Congress Cataloging-in-Publication Data

Tornadoes.
    p. cm. -- (World Book's library of natural disasters)
    Summary: "A discussion of a major type of natural
disaster, including descriptions of some of the most
destructive; explanations of these phenomena, what
causes them, and where they occur; and information
about how to prepare for and survive these forces of
nature. Features include an activity, glossary, list of
resources, and index"--Provided by publisher.
    Includes bibliographical references and index.
    ISBN 978-0-7166-9813-5
    1. Tornadoes--Juvenile literature. 2. Natural disasters--
Juvenile literature.
    I. World Book, Inc.
    QC955.2.T67 2008
    363.34'923--dc22
                        2007015022

World Book's Library of Natural Disasters
Set ISBN: 978-0-7166-9801-2

Printed in China
2 3 4 5 6 12 11 10 09 08

Editor in Chief: Paul A. Kobasa

Supplementary Publications
    Associate Director: Scott Thomas
    Managing Editor: Barbara A. Mayes

Editors: Jeff De La Rosa, Nicholas Kilzer,
    Christine Sullivan, Kristina A. Vaicikonis,
    Marty Zwikel

Researchers: Cheryl Graham, Jacqueline Jasek

Manager, Editorial Operations
    (Rights & Permissions): Loranne K. Shields

Graphics and Design
    Associate Director: Sandra M. Dyrlund
    Associate Manager, Design: Brenda B. Tropinski
    Associate Manager, Photography: Tom Evans
    Designer: Matt Carrington

Product development: Arcturus Publishing Limited
Writer: Neil Morris
Editors: Nicola Barber, Alex Woolf
Designer: Jane Hawkins
Illustrator: Stefan Chabluk

Acknowledgments:

Alamy Images: cover/ title page (A. T. Willett).

AP Photo: 19 (Fred Stewart), 23 (Orlin Wagner), 31 (Pavel Rahman), 41 (The State Gazette/ Chris Rimel).

Center for Severe Weather Research: 36 (Byron Turk).

Corbis: 7, 12 (Eric Nguyen), 8 (Tami Chappell/ Reuters), 9 (M. J. Masotti, Jr./ Reuters), 15, 16 (Jim Reed), 20, 24, 40
    (Reuters), 21 (Sally A. Morgan/ Ecoscene), 22 (Jim Mahoney/ Dallas Morning News), 25 (Corbis Sygma), 26, 27, 29
    (Bettmann), 30 (Andrew Fox), 32 (Jim Zuckerman), 38 (Marc Serota/ Reuters), 42 (Brooks Kraft), 43 (Frank Polich/
    Reuters).

NASA: 33 (Robert Simmon, courtesy of the Global Hydrology and Climate Center).

NOAA: 14 (Jim W. Lee), 37 (wea00206/ Historic NWS Collection), 39 (National Weather Service Storm Prediction Center).

Science Photo Library: 4 (Eric Nguyen), 6 (George Post), 10 (Mike Hollingshead/ Jim Reed Photography), 13 (Aaron
    Johnson & Brooke Tabor/ Jim Reed Photography), 34 (Jim Reed), 35 (David R. Frazier).

TABLE OF CONTENTS

Glossary There is a glossary of terms on pages 45-46. Terms defined in the glossary are in type **that looks like this** on their first appearance on any spread (two facing pages).

Additional resources Books for further reading and recommended Web sites are listed on page 47. Because of the nature of the Internet, some Web site addresses may have changed since publication. The publisher has no responsibility for any such changes or for the content of cited sources.

WHAT IS A TORNADO?

A tornado touches down in Kansas in 2004, sending up a large debris cloud. The tornado was classified as an F3, indicating wind speeds from 158 to 206 miles (254 to 331 kilometers) per hour.

A tornado is an extremely violent windstorm that moves over land. It has stronger winds than any other kind of storm. The winds form under a thundercloud or a developing thundercloud and become a whirling column of air in the shape of a funnel. Tornadoes are sometimes called whirlwinds or twisters because of the spinning nature of the storm. They are one of several spiral-shaped windstorms that **meteorologists** call **cyclones. Hurricanes** and **typhoons,** which form over warm seas, are cyclones, too. Cyclones spin in a counterclockwise direction in the **Northern Hemisphere** and a clockwise direction in the **Southern Hemisphere.**

Where and when tornadoes strike

Although tornadoes can strike in any part of the world, more of them occur in the United States than anywhere else. The United States experiences an average of more than 1,000 tornadoes each year. Tornadoes may strike at any time of day or night. But they occur most often in the afternoon and evening because they are associated with thunderstorms, which form in the warmest part of the day. Most tornadoes in the United States occur in the spring and summer.

How dangerous are they?

Most tornadoes are relatively weak, with wind speeds of less than 110 miles (177 kilometers) per hour. But the most violent tornadoes have wind speeds of more than 300 miles (480 kilometers) per hour. Scientists can sometimes measure a tornado's wind speed with instruments, but generally they estimate wind speed after the tornado has passed by the damage it caused. In the United States, scientists use a system of measurement called the Enhanced Fujita (EF) scale, which has five categories. The wind speeds of hurricanes are also divided into five categories. But the wind speed of the highest category hurricane starts at 156 miles (251 kilometers) per hour. Such a wind speed for a tornado would make it only a category EF3.

Enhanced Fujita scale

Category	Wind speed per hour		Damage description
	(miles)	(kilometers)	
EF0	65–85	105–137	Light
EF1	86–110	138–177	Moderate
EF2	111–135	178–217	Considerable
EF3	136–165	218–266	Severe
EF4	166–200	267–322	Devastating
EF5	Over 200	Over 322	Incredible

T. THEODORE FUJITA

Japanese-born scientist Tetsuya Theodore Fujita (1920–1998) conducted much of his important tornado research at the University of Chicago. He proposed a tornado scale in 1971 and used it to describe and record storms during the 1974 Super Tornado Outbreak. His damage estimates worked so well that the scale was adopted and has since been used to describe every tornado in the United States. Over the years, other researchers found that lower wind speeds can cause more damage than originally thought. During the early 2000's, scientists revised the original F0–F5 Fujita scale. The new Enhanced Fujita scale (EF0–EF5) was adopted in 2007.

The first sign that a tornado is approaching may be light rain. The rain shower is usually followed by heavier rain and then by rain mixed with **hail.** After the hail ends, a tornado may strike. In most cases, a funnel-shaped cloud forms and hangs down from a dark, heavy thundercloud until it touches the ground. However, a tornado can occur even if the funnel does not actually touch the ground.

Thunderclouds

The types of clouds from which tornadoes may develop are called **cumulonimbus** *(KYU myuh loh NIHM bus)* **clouds.** Such clouds may reach as high as 60,000 feet (18,000 meters) above

Hail falls from a cumulonimbus cloud above a desert in Nevada. Hail is a form of precipitation made up of pellets of ice.

the ground. They often have wide, flat tops that resemble the shape of a blacksmith's anvil. Cumulonimbus clouds produce heavy rain, thunder, and lightning as well as hail and tornadoes.

What is hail?

Hailstones are lumps of ice that form inside thunderclouds. They begin as frozen raindrops or snow pellets called *hail embryos.* As the hail embryos are whirled up and down by the fierce winds in a thundercloud, more water freezes around them, making them bigger. Eventually, the hailstones become so heavy that they fall to the ground. Hailstones are often the size of peas, but sometimes they grow as big as golf balls or even softballs. Hail can break windows, damage roofs, and dent cars. It can injure and even kill people, particularly in rural areas where victims may not hear tornado warnings quickly enough to reach shelter.

THE LARGEST HAILSTONES

One of the largest chunks of hail ever to fall in the United States was measured in Aurora, Nebraska, in June 2003. It was 7 inches (18 centimeters) across and weighed 1.3 pounds (0.6 kilogram). The heaviest hailstones on record fell in Bangladesh in 1986. Many of them weighed more than 2 pounds (0.9 kilogram) and reportedly killed 92 people.

A scientist displays a handful of golf-ball-sized hailstones that fell near Moses, New Mexico, in 2003.

THE 2006 TORNADO OUTBREAK

At least 66 tornadoes struck the central United States on the afternoon and evening of April 2, 2006. Six of the tornadoes measured F3—a ranking that indicated severe damage according to the original Fujita scale in effect at that time—with wind speeds of about 200 miles (322 kilometers) per hour. In fewer than 7 hours, the tornadoes killed 26 people and inflicted damage totaling an estimated $193 million. The same area had suffered tornado damage just three weeks earlier.

The Metro Baptist Church in Goodlettsville, Tennessee, is severely damaged from being struck by one of the tornadoes that ripped through the southeastern United States in April 2006.

Moving fast

Meteorologists had forecast that the risk of severe weather would be "moderate" for April 2. The first tornado struck southern Iowa at 3:47 p.m. Huge storms quickly built up and moved south and east. Tornadoes hit Missouri, Arkansas, and

Illinois over the next hour and a half. Almost half of the town of Marmaduke, Arkansas, was destroyed, and nearly every building suffered significant damage. More than a dozen railroad cars were lifted off their tracks and flung into the air. However, no one in the town was killed.

Tragedy in Tennessee

An F3 tornado hit western Tennessee just after 7:30 p.m. It struck the small town of Newbern, where 16 people, many of whom worked at a local food processing plant, were killed. At least 75 others were injured. About 1,000 homes throughout the state were destroyed. Governor Phil Bredesen stated, "I've been through several tornadoes. I'm used to seeing roofs off houses, houses blown over—these houses were down to their foundations, stripped clean." One Newbern resident described being "lifted up in the air and the house was spinning" before the structure was set down 12 feet (4 meters) from its foundation.

A car sits relatively untouched on a showroom floor after a tornado struck a car dealership in Gallatin, Tennessee, in April 2006.

Fading out

Four waves of storms struck Kentucky, beginning in late afternoon and continuing through the evening. One of the storms brought an F3 tornado that touched down near Hopkinsville in southwestern Kentucky at 8:50 p.m., injuring at least 28 people. The last state to be struck was Indiana, where the storms hit Indianapolis near 10:00 p.m. By then, they had left a trail of destruction across seven states.

DERECHOS

In addition to spinning tornadoes, the thunderstorms of April 2, 2006, brought with them widespread, fast-moving winds that blow in a straight line. Such windstorms are called **derechos** (deh RAY chos), from a Spanish word that means straight ahead. Meteorologists recorded wind gusts of up to 130 miles (209 kilometers) per hour from the derechos. These straight-line winds were responsible for the death of one person in Illinois and another in Missouri.

SUPERCELL STORMS

The most damaging tornadoes come from powerful thunderstorms called **supercells.** To form, a supercell must have a good supply of moisture. Such a storm also needs a layer of warm, moist air near the ground and a layer of cooler air above. When two **air masses** with widely different temperatures meet, the **atmosphere** becomes unstable. At the border between the two air masses, called a **front,** warm air begins to flow upward. As it rises, the air cools. The moisture it holds as **water vapor condenses** and forms clouds. The air stops rising at high levels and spreads sideways to form the characteristic anvil shape at the top of a thundercloud.

Starting to spin

Inside a storm cloud, as warm air rises and cool air sinks, they create powerful **air currents** called **updrafts** and **downdrafts.** For a tornado to develop, the winds high up in the cloud must

A supercell thunderstorm forms over Nebraska, producing at least two tornadoes from its rotating mesocyclone.

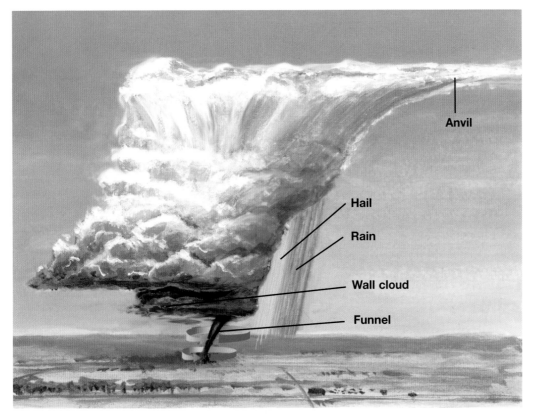

Anvil

Hail

Rain

Wall cloud

Funnel

Most tornadoes are formed by powerful thunderstorms called supercells. Almost all tornadoes in the Northern Hemisphere rotate counterclockwise when viewed from above.

differ from those at lower levels in speed, direction, or both. This difference in wind speed or direction is called **wind shear.** Wind shear makes the column of rising air start to rotate, forming a broad, horizontal tube of swirling air. As the storm continues, this tube starts to tilt until eventually it turns on its end, creating a rotating column of air called a **mesocyclone.**

Producing tornadoes

Meteorologists believe that most supercells that contain mesocyclones eventually produce tornadoes. First, a low, dark, heavy cloud called a **wall cloud** forms underneath the rotating mesocyclone. Tornado funnels develop out of the wall cloud.

INSIDE A THUNDERCLOUD

In 1944, during World War II, a British Wellington bomber took off from an airfield near London. Before long the Royal Air Force plane flew into a cloud at an **altitude** of about 12,000 feet (3,660 meters). The crew soon realized that they were inside a violent thundercloud. The plane was thrown about by winds and bombarded with **hail,** the wings iced up, and finally the plane spun out of control. The Wellington plunged about 7,000 feet (2,130 meters) before the warmer air at the bottom of the cloud melted the ice and the pilot managed to throw the plane out of the thundercloud. Amazingly none of the crew members were injured, and the plane landed safely.

ANATOMY OF A TORNADO

A tornado funnel extends toward the ground near Mulvane, Kansas, in June 2004.

A tornado is a **vortex,** a system of spinning winds similar to a whirlpool formed by swirling water. At the center of the vortex is a calm area called the **eye.** The eye of a tornado may be only a few feet or yards (meters) across. Around the eye, moist air creates a pale cloud in the shape of a funnel. Scientists do not completely understand how a whirling vortex forms. However, they believe that the **updraft** that causes warm air to rise in a **supercell** plays an important role. As the air rises, it creates a **vacuum,** sucking in winds blowing along the ground and perhaps setting them into circular motion. Some tornadoes have more than one vortex swirling around a common center.

On the ground

The funnel acts like the hose of a powerful vacuum cleaner. As it sucks up the winds at ground level, it also begins to pull in dust and dirt from the ground. Soon after it touches the ground, the funnel becomes gray or brown from all of the **debris** it has collected. At its base, the funnel may be very narrow or as much as 1 to 2 miles (2 to 3 kilometers) across. But the size of a tornado does not help forecasters predict how dangerous the twister will be. Very narrow tornadoes are sometimes more destructive than much wider ones.

Traveling along

Supercell storms usually last for several hours as they are pushed through the sky by **prevailing winds** high up in the atmosphere. Their tornadoes travel along with them. Most tornadoes are short-lived, lasting only for about 5 to 10 minutes. However, some have been known to last an hour or more. Tornadoes generally move over the ground at 25 to 35 miles (40 to 56 kilometers) per hour, though some have been clocked at speeds up to 65 miles (105 kilometers) per hour. Few tornadoes travel a distance greater than 25 miles (40 kilometers).

A tornado picks up soil and dust as it moves across farmland in Kansas, turning the funnel brown.

SEEING INSIDE A TORNADO

In 1928, Kansas farmer Will Keller saw a tornado approaching after a **hailstorm.** He ran to his cellar to make sure his family was safe. But just before he joined them and slammed the door, he looked up and saw right inside the tornado's funnel as it passed overhead. "Everything was as still as death," Keller later wrote. "There was a strong gassy odor and it seemed I could not breathe. There was a screaming, hissing sound coming directly from the end of the funnel. ... There was a circular opening in the center of the funnel ... and extending straight upward for a distance of at least one-half mile (800 meters). ... Around the lower rim of the great vortex small tornadoes were constantly forming and breaking away. ... It was these that made the hissing noise."

WATERSPOUTS

A waterspout develops off Key West, Florida, in July 2004. Waterspouts are frequent events in the warm water surrounding the Florida Keys.

When a tornado forms or moves over water, such as a lake, ocean, or even a river, it is called a **waterspout.** Most waterspouts form over warm seas. They are common in summer near the Florida Keys and elsewhere in the Gulf of Mexico and Caribbean Sea. Waterspouts also form along the Atlantic and Pacific coasts of North America and over the Great Lakes. In September and October 2003, 66 waterspouts developed on the Great Lakes over just seven days. On one day alone, 21 waterspouts were spotted over Lake Ontario.

Danger to sailors and fishing crews

Waterspouts form beneath **cumulus** or **cumulonimbus clouds.** Just like tornadoes, waterspouts occur when a cold air mass moves in on top of warm, moist air. Waterspouts appear to suck up water at the bottom of their funnel and carry it up toward the clouds. In fact, the water in the funnel comes from the **condensation** of **water vapor** in the surrounding air. Most waterspouts last for only 2 to 20 minutes. They measure from 20 to 200 feet (6 to 60 meters) across. Even though waterspouts are usually slow moving and most ships can avoid them, they can cause severe damage if they appear suddenly. In May 1980, a waterspout in San Antonio Bay, Texas, sank a shrimp boat. One crew member was lost and two others were injured. Severe tornadoes can also move out over water and become waterspouts. In September 1935, a tornado that formed near Norfolk, Virginia, became a waterspout when it crossed over water and destroyed part of a pier and tossed boats onto the shore. It then became a tornado again and tore some railroad cars off their tracks before heading out into Chesapeake Bay where it became a waterspout again.

Disasters in the 1800's

The *Mary Celeste,* an American sailing ship, was found abandoned in the Atlantic Ocean in November 1872. The disappearance of the captain, his family, and the crew is one of the great unsolved mysteries of the sea. Many researchers have developed theories about what happened to all the people onboard.

According to one theory, a devastating waterspout hit the ship, causing such violent waves that the captain and crew believed the ship was sinking. They may have abandoned ship only to perish in their lifeboat. In the mid-1900's, a **meteorologist** who studied the weather reports at the time that the *Mary Celeste* sailed described what might have happened: "Passage of the waterspout's **vortex** over the vessel would require but a few seconds, the twinkling of an eye, and in that moment the entire ship's company, and the boat they hoped would save them, are swept into the sea, which buries its secret with the dead."

In December 1879, a section of the bridge over the Tay River in Scotland collapsed, and a train that had been traveling over the bridge plunged into the river. All 74 people aboard the train were killed. According to witnesses, two or three waterspouts about 260 feet (79 meters) high had appeared in the river near the bridge just as the train approached. Apparently, they damaged the bridge significantly enough to cause the fatal accident.

LANDSPOUTS AND GUSTNADOS

A **landspout** is a weak tornado that forms beneath a cumulus cloud rather than the cumulonimbus cloud from which **supercell** tornadoes develop. Although a landspout is still a tornado and can cause significant damage and kill people, it usually only produces minor damage, such as breaking tree limbs and destroying small sheds. A **gustnado,** on the other hand, is not a real tornado. It is a weak, short-lived whirlwind caused by gusty ground winds that do not connect with a cloud. Damage from a gustnado is usually limited to broken windows and tree branches or garbage cans and lawn furniture that have been tossed about.

A gustnado spins across the ground in New Mexico. A gustnado is a weak, short-lived whirlwind, which usually causes limited damage.

TORNADO ALLEY

More than 48,000 tornadoes were reported in the United States from 1950 to 2005—an average of 860 each year. Beginning in the mid-1990's, the average increased to more than 1,000 tornadoes per year. The most severe tornadoes—categories F3, F4, and F5—amounted to fewer than 2 percent of all tornadoes. However, these violent twisters caused nearly two-thirds of the 4,716 tornado-related deaths reported from 1950 to 2005. In addition, around 81,000 people were injured by tornadoes.

A tornado strikes near Attica, Kansas, on May 12, 2004, creating a large, dirt-filled debris cloud. Seconds before this photograph was taken, the tornado destroyed a house.

The majority of tornadoes in the United States occur in one of two areas—the state of Florida and a belt known as Tornado Alley. **Meteorologists** do not agree on the exact boundaries of Tornado Alley. However, the belt is generally described as covering an area north from Texas to Nebraska and from Arkansas to Iowa and east through Illinois and Indiana.

Warm air meets cold

Tornado Alley is the site of so many tornadoes because it is the place where two great **air masses** meet. Cool, moist air moves eastward from the North Pacific Ocean. As it is forced upward over the Rocky

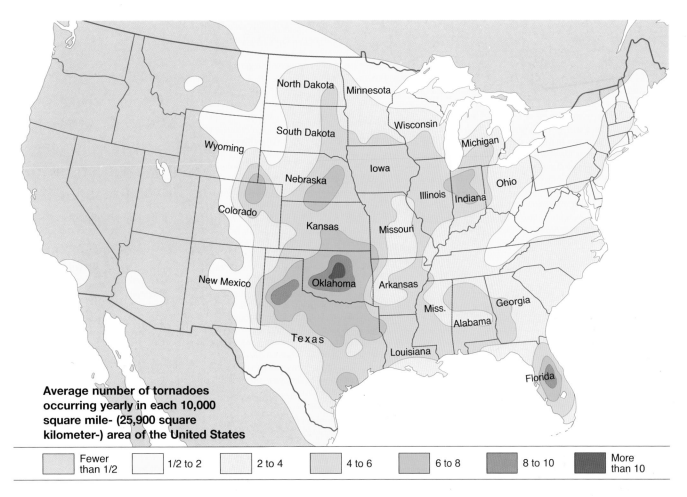

Average number of tornadoes occurring yearly in each 10,000 square mile- (25,900 square kilometer-) area of the United States

| | Fewer than 1/2 | | 1/2 to 2 | | 2 to 4 | | 4 to 6 | | 6 to 8 | | 8 to 10 | | More than 10 |

Mountains, this air mass cools down even more and drops much of its moisture as rain. By the time it reaches the other side of the mountains and blows across the Great Plains, the air is cold and dry. Farther south, warm, moist air moves up from the Gulf of Mexico. It warms up even more as it crosses land before meeting the cold air from the north. The warm air is forced to rise quickly, producing massive thunderclouds and everything associated with them—including tornadoes.

Tornadoes are most common in a belt in the Midwest and South known as Tornado Alley.

WHICH STATES GET THE MOST TORNADOES?

Tornadoes have occurred in every state of the United States. From 1953 to 2004, Texas had the greatest average number of tornadoes per year—139. Oklahoma averaged 57 tornadoes a year, and Kansas and Florida both averaged 55. The next most tornado-prone states were Nebraska, with 45; Iowa, with 37; and Illinois, with 35. Alaska has the fewest number of tornadoes per year. From 1950 to 1995, Alaska had one tornado. It occurred in 1959 and caused minor damage with no reported deaths or injuries.

THE SUPER TORNADO OUTBREAK

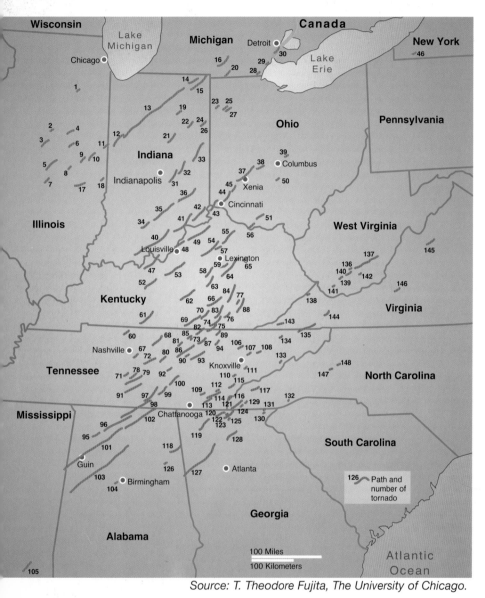

Source: T. Theodore Fujita, The University of Chicago.

The so-called Super Tornado Outbreak of April 3 and 4, 1974, was the largest outbreak ever recorded. A total of 148 twisters hit more than a dozen U.S. states and a Canadian province over a period of 16 hours. The damage path covered more than 2,500 miles (4,000 kilometers) from Illinois and Mississippi in the west to Virginia and New York in the east. More than three-quarters of the tornadoes had paths over 1 mile (1.6 kilometers) long. The longest traveled 121 miles (195 kilometers). Six of the twisters were ranked with an intensity of F5 on the Fujita scale. By the time the storms died down, at least 315 people were dead and about 6,000 others were injured.

All the tornadoes of the 1974 outbreak traveled in a northeasterly direction, cutting parallel tracks through the United States and southern Canada.

Xenia, Ohio

The outbreak began on April 3 in Morris, Illinois, at around 1 p.m. Two and a half hours later, the first F5 tornado struck, about 250 miles (400 kilometers) to the east of Morris, in Xenia, Ohio. There had been 20 tornadoes reported in the central United States on April 1, with several deaths. But people in the town of Xenia had little experience with killer twisters. The town did not even have any warning sirens.

One of the tornadoes that struck Xenia was the deadliest of the outbreak. It traveled at a speed of about 50 miles (80 kilometers) per hour and carried winds estimated from 261 miles (420 kilometers) to 318 miles (512 kilometers) per hour. The twister devastated half the town, destroying 1,300 buildings—including 5 of 10 schools—and damaging 2,000 other structures. Thirty-four people were killed, and about 1,000 others were injured. Just a few miles away, in Wilberforce, Ohio, a **meteorologist** reported seeing an automobile "rolled up into a near perfect ball." Apparently, someone had driven a car directly into the path of the tornado.

A tornado funnel moves through the southeast Pine Crest Garden area of Xenia, Ohio, on April 3, 1974. The F5 tornado killed 34 people in the town.

Other violent twisters

In addition to the F5 tornado that hit Xenia, five other tornadoes with an F5 intensity developed during the outbreak. They struck Brandenburg, Kentucky; Sayler Park, a suburb of Cincinnati, Ohio; Guin, Alabama; Tanner, Alabama; and Depauw, Indiana. The tornado that reached Sayler Park was the only twister of the outbreak to travel through three states. It began in Indiana, crossed the Ohio River, and moved into Kentucky. Then it crossed the river again, travelling into Ohio.

THE LA NIÑA EFFECT

Some meteorologists have suggested that the Super Tornado Outbreak might have been the result of a **climate** effect known as La Niña ("girl child" in Spanish). In a La Niña year— such as 1974—cold, deep-sea water comes to the surface in the eastern Pacific Ocean. The climate becomes wetter than normal in the Pacific Northwest and drier than normal in the southern United States. However, most scientists believe that there are too many variables involved in creating a tornado to make a direct connection between La Niñas and tornadoes.

TORNADO DAMAGE

Before a tornado strikes, no one can predict the damage it will cause. There are no "typical" tornadoes. One twister may tear the roof off a house and collapse its walls, and another tornado may pick up a house, turn it around, and set it down again without any damage. Yet even "weak" tornadoes can be deadly. **Meteorologists** generally measure storms after the event, when damage can be assessed. The Enhanced Fujita scale ranks tornadoes by the damage they cause.

Flying debris

Most deaths and property damage during a tornado are caused by flying **debris.** When a tornado strikes, it picks up such large, heavy objects as cars, trees, and other pieces in its path, whirls them around, and flings them out at an angle. The debris sprays out from the tornado's funnel, smashing into other objects. Scientists who studied tornadoes that occurred in the United States from 1985 to 1997 found that nearly two-thirds of tornado-related deaths occurred in houses or mobile homes.

A rescue worker searches through the remains of mobile homes in a trailer park in Alberta, Canada, after a tornado devastated the park in July 2000, killing nine people and injuring more than 100 others.

Location	Number of deaths 1985–1997	Percentage of total
In a mobile home	230	38
In a permanent home	162	27
In a vehicle	66	11
Outdoors	56	9
At a business address	27	4
Other, unknown	27	4
Under a long-span roof	22	4
At school	15	2
TOTAL	605	100*

*Percentages do not add up to 100 because of rounding.
University of Nebraska-Lincoln High Plains Climate Center.

Wind damage

The winds of a **supercell** storm have devastating power. Before a tornado strikes, violent wind **gusts** usually blow through the area. The spiraling winds of a tornado cause great damage because they are constantly changing direction as the tornado moves over the ground. A wind with a speed of 300 miles (480 kilometers) per hour (category EF5) hits objects with a pressure force of 404 pounds per square foot (1,950 kilograms per square meter). Most homes are designed to withstand pressure of only 50 pounds per square foot (244 kilograms per square meter). A tornado is often followed by severe hail, torrential rain, and more **gale**-force winds.

A dust devil blows across Amboseli National Park in Kenya. Dust devils develop when the layer of air just above the ground is heated by a hot surface.

DUST DEVILS

Dust devils are small, rapidly rotating columns of air that form on clear, hot, dry afternoons in open areas or deserts. Dust devils look similar to tornadoes and may cause damage. However, dust devils are usually much weaker and form in a different way. Dust devils develop when the layer of air just above the ground is heated by a hot surface, such as sand or an asphalt parking lot. The warm air rushes up through the cooler layers above it, creating a **vortex**. The dust devil rises from the surface to heights of 660 feet (200 meters) or more. It does not descend from a cloud, as a tornado does. As it rises, a dust devil carries with it dust and debris from the ground. Dust devil winds have occasionally been recorded at speeds of up to 70 miles (110 kilometers) per hour. Such winds have torn the roofs off buildings, caused small aircraft to roll and crash, and injured and killed people.

Light damage

Tornadoes in the EF0 and EF1 Fujita scale categories are sometimes called "weak" tornadoes. But their wind speeds of up to 110 miles (177 kilometers) per hour can make even so-called light damage significant. From 1997 to 2006, F0 tornadoes caused the deaths of 3 people in the United States, and F1 tornadoes caused the deaths of 45 people. An EF0 tornado may break tree branches, damage roofs, and shatter windows. An EF1 twister may cause mobile homes to be pushed off their foundations. Most of these tornadoes leave damage paths less than 165 feet (50 meters) wide.

Severe damage

EF2 and EF3 tornadoes cause considerable or severe damage. They uproot large trees, so that wooded areas may lose a large percentage of their trees. They tear roofs off houses, sometimes causing outer and inner walls to collapse. They may demolish mobile homes and overturn cars or lift them off the ground.

The damage path of a tornado that touched down in Texas in May 2006 is clearly visible across the earth. The tornado left a path of destruction that extended 10 miles (16 kilometers).

Devastation

Extremely destructive EF4 and EF5 twisters may lift solid, well-built houses off their foundations and demolish them. Cars and such other large objects as trains and trucks may be thrown for more than 300 feet (90 meters). **Debris** is scattered over a wide area. EF4 and EF5 tornadoes may leave a damage path that is 1 to 3 miles (1.6 to 5 kilometers) wide.

Environmental damage

Uprooted trees and plants can leave bare soil. Any additional winds can then cause **dust storms** that wear away the topsoil. A tornado can also cause great environmental damage by striking and picking up such hazardous or **toxic** materials as farm chemicals, landfill trash, medical waste, or even radioactive materials.

SUCTION SPOTS

Some tornadoes contain smaller rotating columns of air called **suction spots** or **suction vortices.** The suction spots revolve around the central **axis** of the tornado. They may last just a few seconds, but they can inflict tremendous damage to small areas. Some experts have suggested that suction spots might be responsible for mysterious crop circles—circular areas of flattened crops sometimes found by farmers in fields.

Fully 95 percent of Greensburg, Kansas, was leveled by a devastating EF5 tornado on May 4, 2007.

Destroyed houses in Oklahoma City along the path of one of the tornadoes that hit Oklahoma and Kansas in May 1999, killing at least 48 people.

A deadly outbreak of 78 tornadoes struck Oklahoma and south-central Kansas from May 3 to 5, 1999. Violent storms killed at least 48 people, injured about 900 others, and damaged more than 12,000 homes. Total damages amounted to more than $1 billion. The biggest twister was an F5 that developed 45 miles (72 kilometers) southwest of Oklahoma City. By the time it reached Oklahoma City, its wind speed had been measured at a record 318 miles (512 kilometers) per hour.

Warnings save lives

May 3 began sunny and warm in Oklahoma. However, the local storm prediction center warned that there was a "slight risk" of severe weather. By late morning, forecasters were calling it a "moderate risk," and by 4 p.m., the warning had been upgraded to "high risk." A tornado watch was issued as the skies grew dark and thunderstorms developed. Tornadoes occurred throughout Oklahoma from late afternoon through the evening. In Oklahoma City, television and radio stations interrupted normal programs to warn people of the direction the storms were heading. Experts later said that these early warnings saved many lives.

Shelter turns deadly

During the Oklahoma outbreak, several people sought shelter under highway overpasses and died as a result. In one instance, 17 people sheltered under an overpass on Interstate 35. All but one of them were blown out of the underpass. After 1999, public safety experts advised people against sheltering under overpasses for two reasons: winds increase in speed and swirl around even more in a confined space; the effect of flying **debris** is much more dangerous in a confined space. According to the U.S. Federal Emergency Management Agency, "Do not get under an overpass or bridge. You are safer in a low, flat location."

A man in Oklahoma City searches for belongings in the debris of his home after the May 1999 Oklahoma tornado outbreak.

FLEEING INTO DANGER

An Associated Press reporter described the experiences of one family who sought shelter under an overpass during the Oklahoma City tornadoes of 1999: "Terry Porter, her husband, Kevin, and their son, Benjamin ... fled their Oklahoma City home toward Interstate 35 on May 3. They made it to an overpass on the east side of the highway and ran up the incline to the ledge beneath the overpass. The wind began sucking their son out, but [his father] was able to shield him. Terry Porter said, 'The next thing I remember is stuff hitting me in the back of the head. ... We were whirling around in there.' Their two-year-old son suffered cuts and bruises; Terry Porter suffered a concussion; and Kevin Porter ... suffered a broken foot, deep lacerations to his arms and other injuries requiring surgery. ... The house was unscathed."

CITY DISASTERS

Supercell thunderstorms form and move over urban areas (towns and cities) as well as over rural areas (the countryside). Because there are many more people and buildings in urban areas, tornadoes often cause much more damage in such places. The tornado outbreak of 1999 struck the southern suburbs of Oklahoma City. In fact, since 1890, more than 100 tornadoes have passed through that city's metropolitan area—more tornadoes than have struck any other city. Other tornadoes have hit even closer to city centers.

St. Louis, Missouri

St. Louis, Missouri, in the heart of Tornado Alley, has been hit many times by severe twisters. The first occurrence on record was in 1871, when a tornado tore Mississippi steamboats apart and killed

A contemporary illustration depicts the scenes of destruction after an F4 tornado struck St. Louis in 1896.

nine people in the city. But the biggest strike came in 1896, when an F4 twister crossed the city's downtown area and left a path of destruction 1 mile (1.6 kilometers) wide through factories, railroad yards, schools, and homes. This tornado left at least 137 people dead before it moved across the river to East St. Louis, where it killed more people. The total death toll was about 255. More than 1,000 people were injured.

In 1927, an F3 tornado tore apart more than 200 St. Louis city blocks and left 72 people dead. **Debris** landed as far away as 50 miles (80 kilometers) from the city. In 1959, 21 deaths in St. Louis were caused by a tornado that also injured 345 people.

LEGEND AND MYTH

Native Americans of the Osage tribe, originally living in Arkansas, Kansas, Missouri, and Oklahoma, passed on many legends. According to one, tornadoes never strike land near the point where two rivers meet. Many people believed this, and it became something of a modern myth. But in both 1974 and 1990, Emporia, a town of nearly 27,000 between the Neosho and Cottonwood rivers in Kansas, was hit by devastating tornadoes. And St. Louis itself lies just 10 miles (16 kilometers) south of where the Mississippi and Missouri rivers meet.

A chaotic scene in Waco, Texas, after a tornado caused a 5-story furniture store in the center of the city to collapse in 1953.

Texas city twisters

In 1953, a two-block-wide F5 tornado struck downtown Waco, Texas. People ran from the streets into stores and offices, but many buildings collapsed. The tornado destroyed more than 850 houses and 600 businesses. Altogether, 114 people died and nearly 600 others were injured. In more recent times, a tornado struck downtown Fort Worth in March 2000. It tore a 3-mile (4.8-kilometer) path through the city.

THE TRI-STATE TORNADO, 1925

The most deadly tornado in U.S. history struck the Midwest on March 18, 1925, killing at least 689 people. It earned its name, the Tri-State Tornado, because it devastated communities in three states. The tornado began in Missouri, crossed Illinois, and ended in Indiana. It took three-and-a-half hours to complete its journey of 219 miles (352 kilometers)—the longest tornado track recorded up to that time. The twister moved at speeds of up to 73 miles (117 kilometers) per hour, damaging 19 communities, destroying 15,000 homes, and leaving more than 2,000 people injured. Eight other tornadoes developed during the same storm, and though they were all weaker, they caused about 60 additional fatalities.

The path of the Tri-State Tornado that began in Missouri, crossed Illinois, and ended in Indiana.

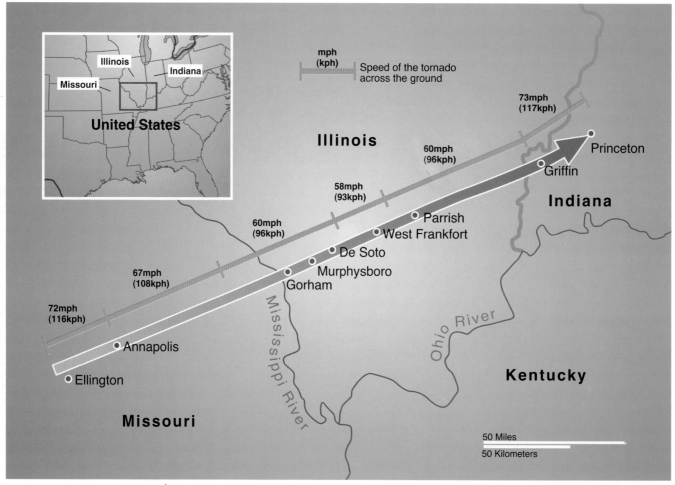

Source: David Jones, Southern Illinois University.

From Missouri to Illinois

The first tornado was sighted at about 1 p.m. in southeastern Missouri. It damaged two schools, killed a child, and injured 32 other children as it moved east and crossed the Mississippi River into Illinois. There it wiped out the small town of Gorham before tearing through Murphysboro, where 234 people lost their lives. A total of 154 of Murphysboro's 200 blocks were destroyed. The situation was made even worse by fire outbreaks. The tornado cut off the town's water supply, so firefighters could only watch helplessly as buildings caught fire from broken gas pipes.

Horror in Murphysboro

At the time, there were few systems to warn people of approaching violent weather. "We didn't even know the word *tornado*," said one Murphysboro survivor. "To us, it was just a storm." Local people were amazed by the violence of the storm. "It was so big; it was so nasty," said another resident. "It just looked like a cloud eating the ground as it went along." Those who survived knew they were lucky to be alive when they saw the destruction. "There was absolutely nothing left," said one survivor. "There's not even foundations. Even a lot of the **debris** was carried away. It just looked like something that was just absolutely scrubbed clean."

FLYING BANKNOTES

In Murphysboro, the winds were so strong that important documents were sucked out of the safe in one man's home. A bond (loan certificate) was later found in the Illinois town of Lawrenceville, about 125 miles (180 kilometers) northeast of Murphysboro. It was returned to its owner by mail. In Robinson, even farther from Murphysboro, a farmer could not believe his eyes when $10 and $20 bills fell out of the sky. They had been blown all the way from the tornado-hit town.

Open-air emergency food stations were set up in Murphysboro, Illinois, to help people made homeless by the 1925 tornado.

Although tornadoes are most frequent in North America, they can occur all around the world. The only continent where they have never been reported is Antarctica, where any kind of thunderstorm is extremely rare. More tornadoes occur in Bangladesh than in any other country outside the United States. Tornadoes also occur fairly frequently in Europe and India. Relatively few tornadoes are reported from Africa or South America.

A car lies against a house in Birmingham in the United Kingdom after a tornado struck the southeast of the city in July 2005.

Bangladesh, 1989

The world's deadliest tornado destroyed Saturia and Manikganj and damaged other towns in central Bangladesh on April 26, 1989. Bangladesh, which lies on the coast of the Bay of Bengal, suffers regularly from **tropical cyclones.** However, at that time, there had been a severe six-month **drought** across the area. The tornado left a path of destruction 8 miles (13 kilometers) long and 1 mile (1.6 kilometers) wide. It destroyed all structures in an area of 2.3 square miles (6 square kilometers) and uprooted and blew away thousands of trees. It left about 1,300 people dead, 12,000 injured, and about 80,000 homeless. According to the *Bangladesh Observer* newspaper, the devastation was so complete in Saturia that all that was left were "skeletons of trees."

Australia, 1970

The most destructive tornado ever reported in Australia passed near the town of Bulahdelah, New South Wales, on Jan. 1, 1970. It left a damage path 14 miles (22 kilometers) long and 1 mile (1.6 kilometers) wide through the Bulahdelah State Forest, destroying more than 1 million trees.

People collect pieces of tin to rebuild their homes in Gopalpur, 95 miles (150 kilometers) north of Dhaka, Bangladesh, after a tornado devastated the region in 1996.

CRASH CAUSE

On Oct. 6, 1981, a short-range Fokker jet airliner took off from Rotterdam Airport in the Netherlands. It was heading for Eindhoven, but just a few minutes into the flight, the aircraft entered the clouds of a thunderstorm and was hit by a tornado. The twister tore off the plane's right wing at an **altitude** of about 3,000 feet (914 meters). The airliner broke up and plunged to the ground. All 13 passengers and 4 crew members were killed.

OTHER HAZARDS

Thunderstorms, especially **supercell** storms, produce other kinds of extreme weather as well as tornadoes. Lightning may be seen in the distance as a thunderstorm approaches. As a storm passes overhead, the severe winds are usually followed by **hail,** which can also cause great damage. Then comes torrential rain, which can produce **flash floods.**

Lightning

Lightning often occurs during the formation of a **wall cloud.** Scientists believe that electric charge builds up in thunderclouds as rising water droplets and tiny pieces of ice collide with hail and other heavier, falling particles. Eventually, the charge becomes so powerful that an electric spark surges from one part of the cloud to another or from the cloud to the air, to another cloud, or to the ground. Lightning that strikes the ground causes about 1,000 deaths around the world each year. According to the U.S. National Weather Service, lightning killed an average of 61 people per year in the United States from 1977 to 2006— 7 more fatalities than the average number of deaths caused by tornadoes during the same period. Lightning strikes can also cause fire.

Lightning is accompanied by thunder—the explosive noise caused by the violent expansion of air that has been heated by lightning. Because of this connection, the National Weather Service uses the slogan "When thunder roars, go indoors!"

A violent thunderstorm produces both lightning and a tornado.

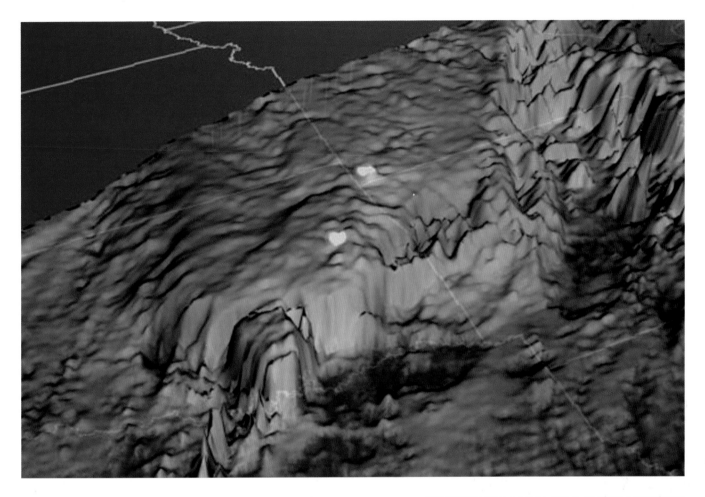

Lightning flashes in storms over Oklahoma in October 1998 are overlaid on cloud-top data from a satellite image. The frequency of the lightning flashes in the heaviest storm areas helps scientists assess the potential for tornado formation.

Flash floods

Most flash floods are caused by slow-moving thunderstorms or by thunderstorms that move repeatedly over the same area. Such floods can develop within minutes, catching people unawares. On average, 99 people in the United States died annually in flash floods from 1977 to 2006, nearly twice the average number of tornado deaths. Flooding can cause additional damage to areas already affected by tornadoes.

LIGHTNING MAPPING ARRAY

Scientists have learned that lightning often provides clues about which storms will become the most severe. They have set up radio receivers in Alabama, Florida, New Mexico, Oklahoma, Texas, and Washington, D.C., that measure and record the time of arrival of lightning flashes to within less than a millionth of a second. A computer then maps the lightning activity, showing the source of the lightning as well as each lightning strike. **Meteorologists** hope to use the information from these arrays to issue more accurate—and more timely—warnings of severe storms.

Tornadoes are unpredictable, but **meteorologists** have learned to forecast severe storms and give general warnings. They can often predict severe weather 12 to 48 hours in advance. They use information from **weather balloons** high in the atmosphere, **satellites** orbiting Earth, and **radar** devices on the ground. All this information is fed into computers, which can present an overall picture of the situation on a weather map. Once a tornado has appeared, scientists can track its progress and let people know if it is heading their way.

Doppler effect

Meteorologists use a special system called Doppler radar to look for **mesocyclones** and tornadoes. The system is based on the fact that **radio waves** change their **frequency** (rate of vibration) depending on whether the objects they bounce off, such as raindrops, are moving toward or away from the radar device. This change in frequency, called the **Doppler effect,** reveals the spinning winds of a tornado.

A Doppler radar image allows meteorologists in Kansas to monitor a storm. The different colors represent varying intensities of rainfall.

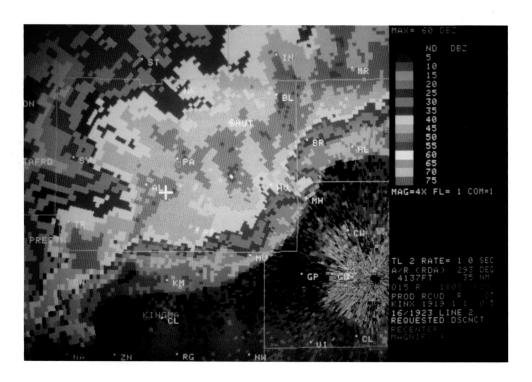

Radar network

The U. S. National Storm Prediction Center has a network of about 160 Doppler radar sites located throughout the United States and overseas. This network is called NEXRAD (for next-generation weather radar) and is used to measure **precipitation** and wind. Each of the devices looks like a giant golf ball mounted on a steel tower. The NEXRAD devices transmit a continuous radio wave of a constant frequency. When the wave strikes an approaching object—such as a raindrop, **hail,** or a speck of dust—it is reflected back at a higher frequency than the one at which it was sent out. When an object is moving away from the set, the wave is bounced back at a lower frequency. The faster an object moves in either direction, the greater the difference between the transmitted and reflected frequencies. By measuring this difference, Doppler radar can determine the wind speed of tornadoes, the structure and boundary of storms, and the severity of precipitation.

CHRISTIAN DOPPLER

Austrian physicist Christian Doppler (1803–1853) noticed that the pitch of a train whistle seems to sound higher as the train approaches and lower as it moves away. He discovered that the actual pitch remains constant but that the frequency of the sound waves changes depending on the movement of the train toward or away from the observer. As the train moves toward the observer, the sound waves are crowded together and sound higher. As it moves away, the sound waves are spread out and sound lower. In 1842, he presented a set of mathematical equations to support his theory, and the effect was eventually named after him.

A Doppler weather radar tower located south of Boise, Idaho, is part of the NEXRAD network.

STORM CHASERS

Most people want to avoid tornadoes and probably hope they never see one. But storm chasers are professional tornado hunters, and they feel exactly the opposite way. They spend their time studying the weather near where they live and work, mostly in the Tornado Alley area, ready to rush out at a moment's notice. Their dangerous job is to try to get close enough to a tornado to observe and record it.

Doppler on wheels

Meteorologists form mobile teams of storm chasers. They travel in specially equipped cars and trucks as they try to get near tornadoes without coming too close. **Doppler radar** helps them to map wind speed and direction and to study the changes that take place in a thunderstorm before a tornado forms. Some vehicles have radar equipment on board. The U.S. Center for Severe Weather Research has mobile units in its project called "Doppler on wheels." One of these units measured the world-record wind speed during the Oklahoma tornado outbreak of 1999.

A mobile Doppler radar truck allows meterologists to track and chase storms.

TOTO and turtles

Storm chasers try to drop instruments in or near the paths of tornadoes to measure such variables as wind and temperature. They also film flying **debris** so they can later analyze wind patterns. In 1979, meteorologists built a barrel of instruments called TOTO (for *T*otable *T*ornado Observatory), named after Dorothy's dog in *The Wonderful Wizard of Oz.* Placing TOTO in the path of a tornado was a hazardous task, and in 1986, TOTO was replaced by smaller, round instrument-containing devices called *turtles.* Several turtles have been successfully placed in the paths of approaching tornadoes and have recorded valuable information.

An image taken 22 miles (35 kilometers) southwest of Howard, South Dakota, on Aug. 28, 1884, is believed to be the oldest known photograph of a tornado.

AT THE MOVIES

The 1996 action film *Twister* showed storm chasers in action and used special effects to show what a tornado looks like up close. The film's tagline was "The dark side of nature." But perhaps the most famous story involving a tornado was *The Wonderful Wizard of Oz,* written by L. Frank Baum and published in 1900. In the book, a Kansas farm girl named Dorothy and her house are carried by a tornado to a magical land. Baum wrote, "The house whirled around two or three times and rose slowly through the air. Dorothy felt as if she were going up in a balloon." At one time, Baum, who had worked as a reporter, ran a paper called the *Aberdeen Saturday Pioneer* in South Dakota. Just a few years earlier, a photographer had captured the first image ever taken of a tornado near Howard, South Dakota, not very far away. People have wondered whether Baum may have seen the photo of the tornado and been inspired to include a tornado in his book.

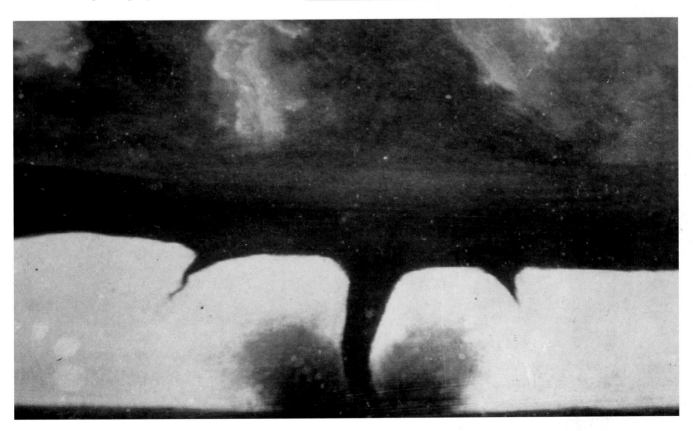

TORNADO WATCH AND WARNING

A thunderstorm descending on Tampa, Florida, in August 2004 prompts the National Weather Service to place the Tampa metropolitan area under a tornado watch. A tornado watch means that conditions make a tornado possible.

In the United States, the National Weather Service issues a tornado watch when there is a likelihood of severe thunderstorms that could produce tornadoes. When a tornado watch is issued, people are alerted to watch for threatening weather and to listen to the radio or TV for more information. A tornado watch means: "Tornadoes are possible in your area. Remain alert for approaching storms."

Moving to the next stage

If **Doppler radar** detects a **mesocyclone** in a thunderstorm or a developing tornado has been reported by a trained storm spotter, the National Weather Service issues a tornado warning. It also issues a warning if someone actually sees a funnel cloud. A tornado warning is a very urgent message that means:

"A tornado has been sighted or indicated by weather radar. If the sky becomes threatening, move to your predetermined place of safety."

Getting the message

Local offices of the National Weather Service issue watches and warnings for tornadoes and severe thunderstorms for counties or parts of counties. The warnings are given to radio and TV stations and are put on the Internet. Average warning times have doubled in recent years from about 5 minutes in the early 1990's to about 11 minutes in the mid-2000's, giving people more time to make themselves safe. These warnings have helped the U.S. tornado death rate go down from 1 person in every 556,000 per year in 1925 to 1 person in every 8.3 million per year in 2000.

Weather radio

Local radio and TV stations give weather updates. In the United States, many people own special Weather Radio All Hazards receivers. Such receivers allow people to hear information transmitted directly from the National Weather Service. The best versions have a tone alarm, which sounds and turns the radio on when there is a severe weather warning.

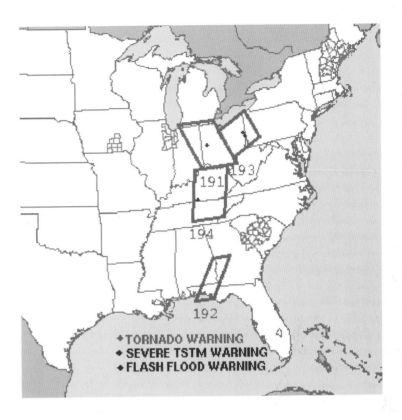

A National Weather Service map gives warning of tornadoes (red), thunderstorms (blue), flash floods (green), and high winds (brown) in the eastern United States in April 2007.

THE FIRST TORNADO FORECAST

During the early evening of March 25, 1948, a tornado roared across Tinker Air Force Base on the outskirts of Oklahoma City. It did great damage but not as much as a twister that had struck the base five days earlier. A few hours before the March 25 tornado struck, Captain Robert C. Miller and Major Ernest J. Fawbush recognized similar conditions and issued a tornado warning. After the first tornado, the two **meteorologists** had been asked to study the weather conditions present that day and to identify a pattern that might indicate a tornado. Aircraft were rolled into hangars and people left dangerous places such as the control tower. This was the first successful tornado warning.

SHELTER FROM THE STORM

Windows of the Bank One Building in Fort Worth, Texas, shattered by two tornadoes that struck the city in March 2000. People are advised to stay away from windows during a tornado because of the danger from broken glass.

The best way to stay safe and survive a tornado strike is to have a well-rehearsed emergency plan. In the United States, the National Severe Storms Laboratory (based in Norman, Oklahoma, in Tornado Alley) and the American Red Cross give specific advice about what to do.

Before the storm

Everyone should know the safest place to go at home, school, or in the work place if a tornado watch or warning is issued. Such a place could be the basement or a central hallway, bathroom, or closet on the lowest floor of the building. People in a high-rise may not have enough time to reach the lowest floor. In this case, they should head for a hallway or similar place in the middle of the building.

A road map is a big help in following storm movements from weather bulletins. People should listen to the radio and watch television for information. Before going out, listen to the latest forecasts and take necessary action if threatening weather is approaching.

Following a warning

When a warning is issued, people should go to the safest place in their home and get under a sturdy piece of furniture, such as a heavy table. Stay away from windows, because of the danger of flying glass. Do not open any windows, because you may allow damaging winds into the house. People used to think that opening windows as a tornado approaches would equalize **atmospheric pressure** inside and outside the building, therefore reducing damage. But experts say that windows should be kept tightly closed. People who live in mobile homes should leave immediately and seek shelter elsewhere.

People who are outdoors in a car should not try to outrun a tornado. Instead, they should stop the car and leave it immediately. If possible, they should go to the basement of a nearby sturdy building. Otherwise, the best plan is to lie flat, facedown, in a ditch or a low-lying area and cover the head. People should not take shelter under a bridge or an overpass.

DISASTER SUPPLIES KIT

People should keep emergency supplies ready. These should include

■ A three-day supply of water—1 gallon (3.8 liters) per person per day

■ Food that won't spoil (dry or canned)

■ Change of clothing and footwear for each person

■ Blanket or sleeping bag per person

■ First-aid kit, including prescription medicines

■ Emergency tools

■ Battery-powered radio, flashlight, and extra batteries

■ Special items for infant, elderly, or disabled family members

Students at Lara Kendall Elementary School in Ridgely, Tennessee, practice a tornado drill in the building's central hallway. The concrete walls and ceiling are reinforced with steel to withstand the force of a tornado.

EMERGENCY SERVICES

Some communities in the United States have public storm shelters. These are useful for people who live close enough to be able to reach the shelter in time after a warning. In Mississippi, 60 community shelters were built after a devastating tornado outbreak there in February 2001. Most of the shelters are in or near fire and police departments or emergency operations centers. During all tornado warnings since 2001, the shelters have been full. In Oklahoma City, residents can register their own private storm shelters on a special Web site. If people become trapped by debris in a registered shelter, emergency service workers would be able to locate them.

After a Federal Emergency Management Agency briefing in 2003, President George W. Bush greets residents of Pierce City, Missouri, at a shelter set up to provide relief for those affected by a tornado that ripped through the neighborhood.

Helping the victims

All over the world, national and local emergency services are ready to help people after a disaster. In the United States, the efforts are coordinated by the Federal Emergency Management Agency (FEMA). The American Red Cross, the Salvation Army, and other volunteer organizations also offer assistance. All these organizations provide food, shelter, and supplies as well as help in cleanup efforts. Such aid was needed in central Florida in February 2007, when tornadoes struck in the middle of the night. The tornadoes damaged 1,500 homes and left at least 20 people dead. The Red Cross and other volunteer groups quickly sent in relief workers, emergency response vehicles, and mobile feeding units.

After the storm

Rescue workers who have come out to help victims after a tornado has passed through an area have witnessed some remarkable sights. In June 1958 near Eldorado, Kansas, a woman who had been pulled through a window of her house by the winds was found lying some 60 feet (18 meters) away, next to a phonograph recording of the popular song "Stormy Weather." During the Oklahoma City tornado outbreak of 1999, a woman, her boyfriend, and her young son took shelter in a bathtub and held a mattress over their heads. As the tornado passed overhead, it tore the roof off their home and dropped a car onto the bathtub. The car caused some injuries to the woman, but it also apparently deflected other **debris,** because all three survived.

A firefighter comforts a resident of Utica, Illinois, after a tornado devastated the town in April 2004.

RAINING FROGS

For many years, people have reported cases of strange objects dropping from the sky after a tornado or **waterspout** outbreak. For example, frogs were reported falling like hailstones in Kansas City, Missouri, in 1873; in Cairo, Illinois, 10 years later; and as recently as 2005, in a small town in Serbia. These incidents are something of a mystery, but many scientists believe that the frogs were picked up by tornadoes or waterspouts and carried long distances high in the sky before being dropped to Earth. There are also tales of other small animals raining down, such as fish, snails, turtles, and worms—in some cases, the entire contents of small ponds!

MAKE YOUR OWN VORTEX

Here is a simple experiment that shows how a tornado works. You are really creating a swirling **vortex** in the form of a whirlpool instead of a whirlwind.

Equipment

- 2 large plastic soft-drink bottles with screw-top lids
- Strong glue
- Food coloring
- Hole punch or drill

1. Remove the screw-top lids from the two bottles. Glue the tops of the lids together. Ask an adult to help you punch or drill a hole the size of a drinking straw through the middle of the lids.

2. Fill one of the bottles about three-fourths full of water. Add some food coloring to make the water currents easier to see. Screw the lids onto the full bottle, and then screw the empty bottle on top. Make sure that the lids are screwed tightly and that the seal is waterproof.

3. Turn the bottles over so that the one with water is on top. Spin them so that the water starts to rotate inside. As the water twists down into the empty bottle, the air will rise up through the water in the top bottle and look just like a tornado.

The air in the bottle represents warm air rising to form a tornado. Try turning the bottle upside down without spinning it. You'll see that the water does not flow through the hole very easily when the bottle is not spinning.

air current A flow of air in a particular direction.

air mass A body of air at a particular temperature, humidity, and height.

altitude A measure of height above Earth's surface or sea level.

atmosphere The layer of gases surrounding Earth.

atmospheric pressure The weight of the air pressing down on Earth's surface.

axis The imaginary line around which something turns.

climate The average weather in an area over a period of time.

condense To change from a gas to a liquid as a result of cooling.

cumulus Heaped up piles of clouds that often look like cotton balls.

cumulonimbus cloud A massive, vertical cloud formation, often with a flat top.

cyclone A violent, swirling windstorm or the weather system in which such windstorms form.

debris Rubble, broken objects, and other damaged material.

derecho A storm with violent winds that blow in a straight line.

Doppler effect The change in frequency of radio waves when they move toward or away from a radar receiver.

downdraft A downward movement of air.

drought A long period of unusually dry weather.

dust storm A strong wind that carries fine particles of earthy material for long distances.

eye The relatively calm area at the center of a hurricane or tornado.

flash flood A sudden, intense flood of a river or lake.

frequency The rate of vibration of a wave such as a radio wave.

front In a weather system, the place where two masses of air meet.

gale A very strong wind; technically, any wind with a speed of 32 to 63 miles (51 to 101 kilometers) per hour.

gust A sudden, violent rush of wind.

gustnado A whirlwind caused by gusty winds on the ground.

hail Pellets of ice that may fall from thunderclouds.

hurricane A tropical storm over the North Atlantic Ocean, the Caribbean Sea, the Gulf of Mexico, or the Northeast Pacific Ocean.

landspout A weak tornado that forms over land.

mesocyclone A rotating column of air that forms inside a thundercloud and can produce tornadoes.

meteorologist A scientist who studies and forecasts weather.

Northern Hemisphere The half of Earth that is north of the equator.

precipitation Moisture that falls from clouds, such as rain, snow, or hail.

prevailing wind The usual wind experienced in a particular place.

radar An electronic instrument that allows weather forecasters to locate areas of rain or snow and track the motion of air in a weather system.

radio wave An electromagnetic wave within certain frequencies.

satellite An object that continuously orbits Earth or some other body in space. People use artificial satellites for such tasks as collecting data.

Southern Hemisphere The half of Earth that is south of the equator.

suction spot (suction vortex) Small rotating columns of air within a tornado.

supercell A powerful, long-lasting thunderstorm that often produces heavy rain, hail, and tornadoes.

toxic Poisonous.

tropical cyclone A violent storm that starts in the tropics.

typhoon A tropical storm in the Northwest Pacific Ocean.

updraft An upward movement of air.

vacuum An empty space without even air.

vortex A spinning column of air at the center of a whirlwind.

wall cloud A low, dark, heavy cloud that forms underneath a mesocyclone.

water vapor Water in the form of a gas.

waterspout A tornado that forms or moves over water.

weather balloon A balloon designed to rise through the atmosphere carrying instruments for measuring the weather at high altitudes.

wind shear A sudden change of wind speed or direction that occurs over a short distance.

BOOKS

Storm Warning: Tornadoes, by Chris Oxlade, Raintree, 2005.

Terrifying Tornadoes, by Louise and Richard Spilsbury, Heinemann Library, 2004.

Tornado Alert! by Wendy Scavuzzo, Crabtree Publishing, 2004.

Tornadoes, by Michael and Mary Woods, Lerner Publications, 2007.

Tornadoes: Disaster and Survival, by Bonnie J. Ceban, Enslow Publishers, 2005.

WEB SITES

http://nationalgeographic.com/ngkids/0306/

http://www.fema.gov/hazard/tornado/index.shtm

http://www.hprcc.unl.edu/nebraska/tornado-myths.html

http://www.noaawatch.gov/themes/severe.php

http://www.weather.gov/om/reachout/tornadoes.shtml

http://www.weatherwizkids.com/tornado.htm

INDEX